plants & flowers
in lace

plants & flowers
in lace

Edited by Bridget M. Cook

B T Batsford Ltd, London

Publisher's Acknowledgement
The publishers would like to acknowledge the contribution of Bridget M. Cook to this book, in both its overall compilation and co-ordination, and the production of the prickings and working diagrams.

Liz Tibbetts contributed greatly to the concept, and publishers would like to acknowledge her involvement both then and in the assembly of the book.

First published 1995

© B.T. Batsford Ltd 1995

ISBN 0 7134 7790 3

Designed by Peter Higgins
Printed in Hong Kong

A CIP record for this title is available from the British Library

Contents

List of contributors and their patterns   6

The international colour-coding system   7

Helpful hints on presentation   7

The patterns

Torchon Flower Mat by Rosanne McLean   10

Katie's Rose by Alison Dews   12

Gold Rush Daisy (*Gerbera jamesonii*)
by Jean Horne   14

Bruges Flowered Mats
by Jacqueline Swinnen-Rosiers   16

Floral Corsage - 3-D Flower
by Radmila Zuman   20

Tulip Cushion by Helene Schou   22

Souvenir de Saint François Picture
by Marie-Christine Gosse   24

Sunflower by Bridget M. Cook   26

Red Poinsettia by Bridget M. Cook   28

Bridesmaid's Posy by Bridget M. Cook   30

Wild Rose Motif by Bridget M. Cook   32

Flowered Handkerchief by Pat Milne   34

Wheat Ear Earrings by Glenda Howell   36

Small White Rose Flower Motif
by Glenda Howell   37

Flower Miniatures by Liz Tibbetts   38

Harebells by Liz Tibbetts   40

Daisy Chains by Liz Tibbetts   42

Tiny Fruits and Flowers by Liz Tibbetts   44

Tulips by Liz Tibbetts   46

Sources of information   48

List of contributors

Liz Tibbetts:	Flower Miniatures
	Snowdrop
	Toadstool
	Daffodil
	Daisy Chains
	Tiny Fruits and Flowers
	Strawberry
	Cherries
	Pear
	Snowdrop
	Mushroom
	Leaf and Tendril
	Harebells
	Tulips
Rosanne McLean:	Torchon Flower Mat
Alison Dews:	Katie's Rose
Jacqueline Swinnen-Rosiers:	Flowered Mats
Jean Horne:	Gold Rush Daisy
Radmila Zuman:	3-D Flower
Helene Schou:	Tulip Cushion
Marie-Christine Gosse:	Souvenire de Saint François
Bridget M. Cook:	Wild Rose
	Bridal Posy
	Poinsettia
	Sunflower
Pat Milne:	Flowered Handkerchief
Glenda Howell:	Wheat Ear Earrings
	Small flower motif

The international colour-coding system

The drawings for all the projects in the Batsford Lace Library have been prepared using the colour-coding system that has been established as the world standard:

Red: Clothstitch and twist (cross, twist, cross, twist) Wholestitch and twist

Purple: Clothstitch (cross, twist, cross) Wholestitch

Green: Halfstitch (cross, twist)

Yellow: The movement of an individual thread. This colour is frequently used to indicate the movement of a gimp thread.

Blue: A two-pair plait

Black: A coarse pair is a mixed threaded pair with one thread thicker than its partner, which is the same thread as used in the rest of the lace. This pair outlines the lace.

Helpful hints for presentation

Mounting lace onto fabric

Select a cloth of a similar weight and feel as the work when mounting the lace.

To attach the lace choose the thread used to create the work or one slightly thicker (and therefore stronger), especially if it is very fine. Choose a needle compatible with the work. A very fine oversewing stitch is the simplest when attaching lace to an existing hem.

Be warned that ready-made handkerchiefs and traycloths may not be truly square or rectangular. The lace should be made to fit the longest side and it can be then gently eased onto any slightly shorter sides. Care should be taken when mounting onto fabric without a hem that the pinholes lie correctly on the weave of the material. For straight edges it is sensible to draw a thread. Pin and tack carefully and attach into every hole of the footside using mock hem stitch, four-sided stitch or a triangular stitch.

On completion of the sewing cut carefully close to the edge. For extra strength and for particularly fine work do not cut too closely. Either roll carefully and whip back the raw edge or, alternatively, make a second row of four-sided stitch. Use a backing of coloured paper for very fine lace and for attaching to net. This will keep the lace in its correct shape and will help to identify the holes for sewing. Pin and tack the lace right-side-down on the paper and then tack the net on top. Oversew the lace to the net, including any motifs inside the border. Then remove the paper and cut the net close to the edge.

Mounting in frames or purpose-bought mounts

Use a small scrape of clear-drying general-purpose PVA adhesive dabbed onto the back of a denser part of the work. Secure the work to the chosen backing material and assemble the frame. Glass, perspex and thick clear PVC film (acetate) are all suitable to protect the work.

Antique frames can often be found and one should always be on the lookout for these. They can be very satisfying and particularly suitable for lace work. Modern purpose-made craft mounts can be in the form of trinket boxes, jewellery, frames, key rings and powder compacts. They all have different methods of holding the craft work in place but all should come with clear instructions.

For paperweights, wedge with a spacer of thick dark card under the lace and its backing, if needed to keep the work from slipping, and finish with a disc of sticky-backed suede vinyl.

Special mounts can be expensive but most designs can be mounted just as effectively on ready-cut cards. Many shapes and sizes are available including bookmarks, gift tags and shapes of sufficient size for large pictures. The best will have a ready-cut aperture behind which the design is fixed with a double fold of card so that the fixing of the work is obscured. For a professional finish protect the work with a thin clear PVC sheet cut slightly larger than the aperture and glued to the back of it.

Different backings of card or fabric can create different results and add an ingredient to the gift or occasion. Silk or velvet is luxurious, but beware of deep pile for fine work as the lace can sometimes move with the pile if handled.

Other ideas for mounting lace

For a permanent and durable finish iron on clear protective coverings as used for covering pressed flowers, in satin matt finish. This seals directly onto most flat surfaces and is ideal for finishing wood mounts such as clock faces, boxes or small wood blocks for making brooches or pendants.

Lace made with thicker thread does not necessarily need to be mounted or covered. Mats and bookmarks can be stiffened with a weak solution of starch or ironed with spray starch. In order to avoid squashing the work place the right side down onto a soft pad and press lightly. A special preparation, such as the stiffener used to make roller blinds, can be used to stick and seal lace to a backing fabric or to stiffen the piece from a light finish to one that is rock-hard. In this way small pieces of work can be stiffened to make jewellery. In order to avoid clogging or opaqueness use thinned and apply several coats until the desired stiffness is obtained. Stiffeners are also required for any 3-D work or lace that is to be hung. This can include a wall or window hanging as it also protects the lace from dust and dirt.

Many of the mounts and fixings can be found in craft suppliers', model shops, florists' and stationers'. Seek out something different, and be inventive in order to create that special lace gift for family or friends.

Torchon Flower Mat

Rosanne McLean USA

Bobbins: 36 pairs
Gimp: 3 pairs
Thread: Fresia linen 80/2
          Cotton Perlé 8 for gimp
          The leaves have a twisted worked vein

Katie's Rose

Alison Dews UK

A mixed lace hexagon
Bobbins: 35 pairs
Gimps: 2 pairs of gimps for each section
Thread: Bouc 140/2 linen (no longer available)
         DMC Perlé 12 for gimp

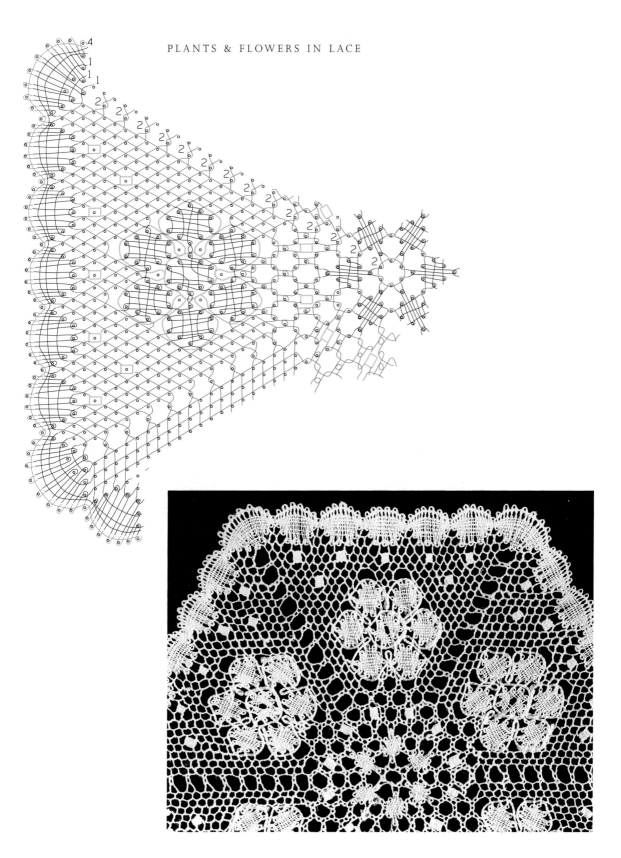

Gold Rush Daisy (*Gerbera jamesonii*)

Jean Horne South Africa

Thread: DMC Turbino Ecru
or DMC 30 machine embroidery

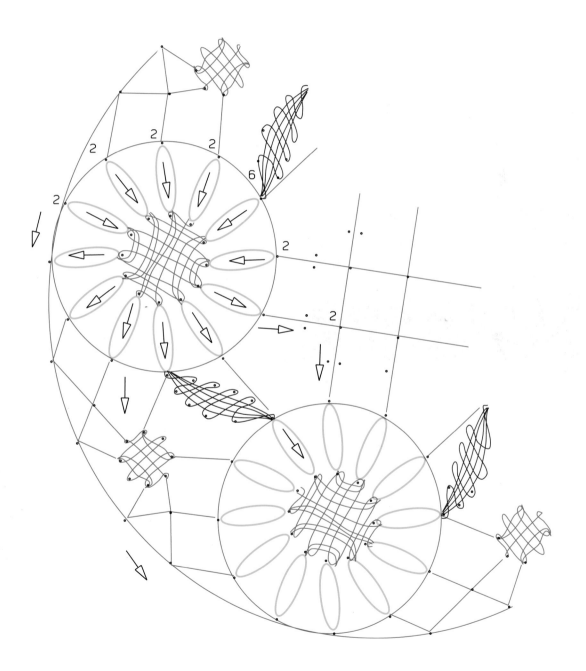

Bruges Flowered Mats

Jacqueline Swinnen-Rosiers Belgium

Four multi-positional elements
Thread: 100/2 linen throughout

*These can be assembled in any combination at
the choice of the maker to produce individual
gifts of varying size and design.*

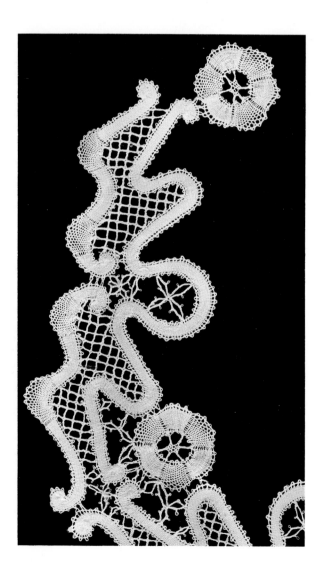

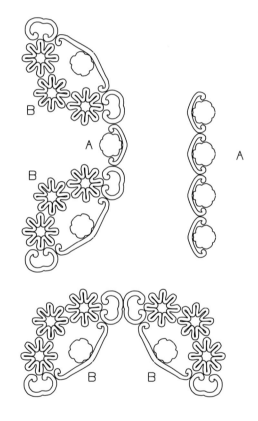

Bruges Flowered Mats (continued)

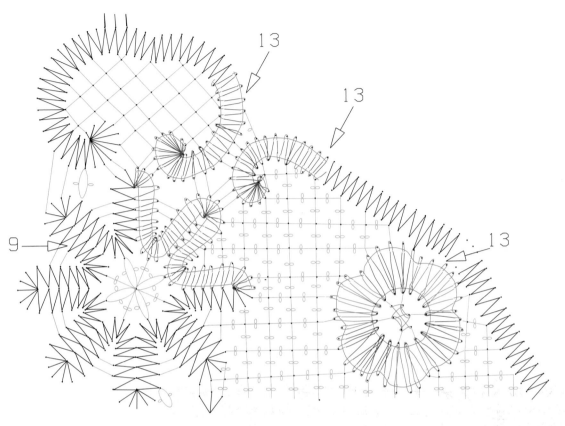

13

13

9

13

Floral Corsage 3-D Flower

Radmila Zuman USA

A: Bobbins:10 pairs 2 pairs for braids
B: Bobbins: 9 pairs 2 pairs for braids
C: Bobbins: 2 pairs with one pair being
mixed with a thicker thread for one bobbin
Thread: Coats Dual Duty Button Thread
Cotton-covered polyester

*Work all three sections, join attractively
together on a pin and stiffen.*

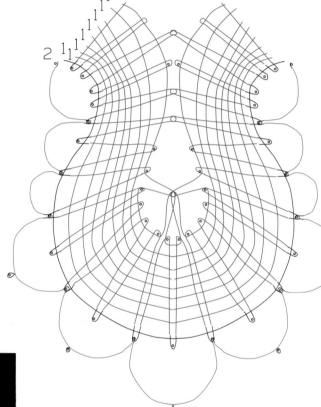

A

C

B

Tulip Cushion

Helene Schou Denmark

Bobbins: 5 pairs for the flowers
Thread: Guttemans coloured silk
or flower cotton

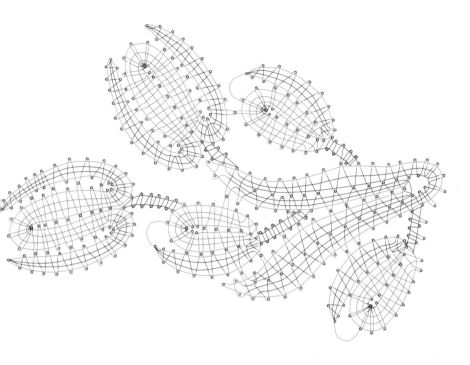

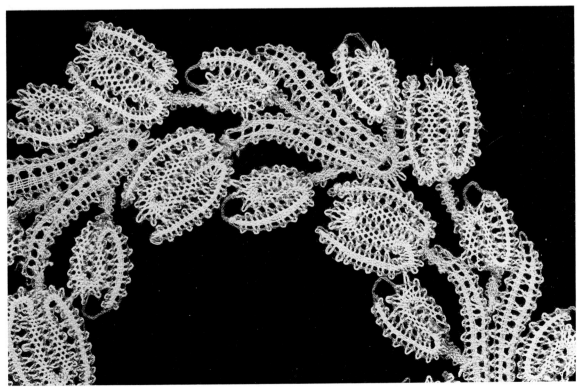

Souvenir de Saint François

Marie-Christine Gosse France

Thread: DMC 80 Special Dentelles

*1. First work the outer border, then the
mountains. Add the ground with sewings onto
the border already made. Simultaneously make
the flowers with the ground pairs as passives.
2. Add the stem when necessary.
Simultaneously work the ground and flowers.
3. Finish up with the cloth-stitch braid.
4. Sew up. Stiffen and mount.*

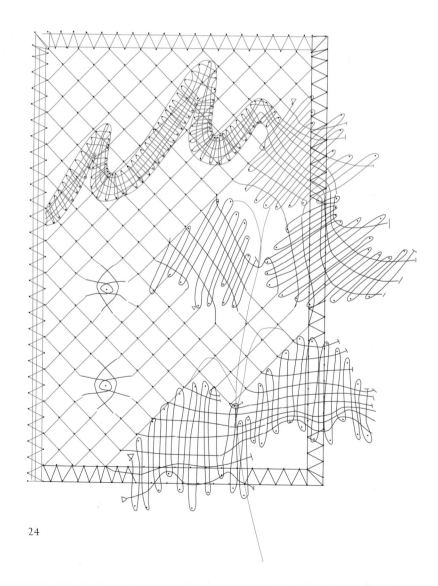

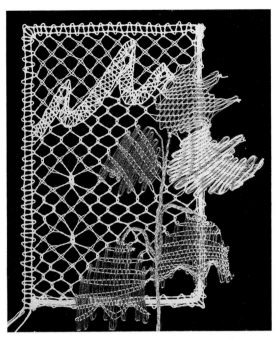

Sunflower

Bridget M. Cook UK

Bobbins: 16 pairs
Thread: DMC 80 Special Dentelles
This can be made in two colours, 14 of one
and 2 of the other: the worker pair for the fan
and the outside passive pair.

*Start in the middle, adding pairs
towards the edge. Work the fan
and then work down to the middle.
Continue in this manner.*

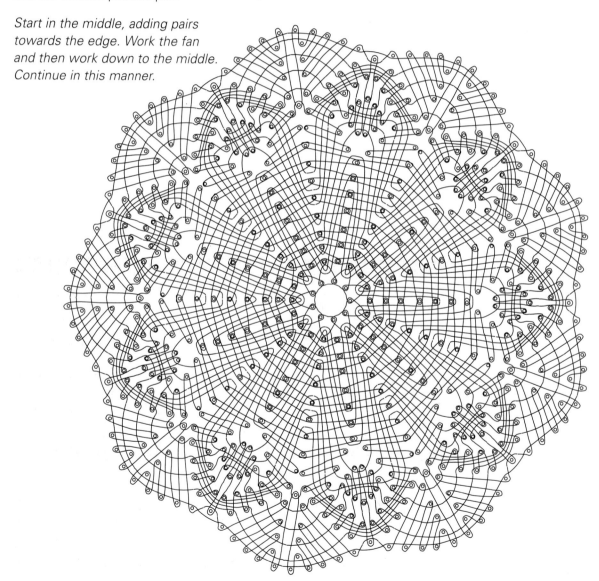

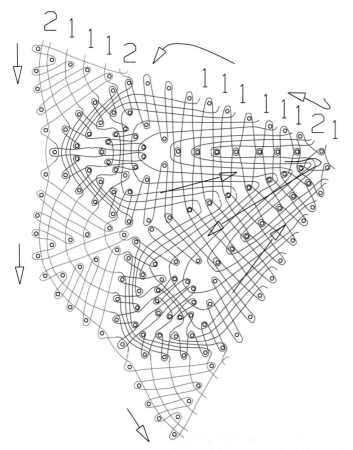

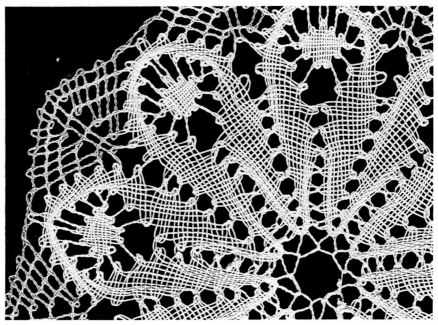

Red Poinsettia

Bridget M. Cook UK

Bobbins: 15 pairs
Thread: DMC 80 Special Dentelles

*Start in the middle and work up and
down for each petal.*

Bridesmaid's Posy

Bridget M. Cook UK

Bobbins: 25 pairs
          1 pair of gimps
Thread: Tanné 80
        Perlé 8 for the gimp

*These attractive circles may be used as mats
or can be gathered and sewn on to a plastic
posy holder to set off a small bouquet.*

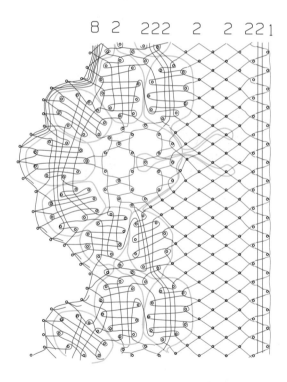

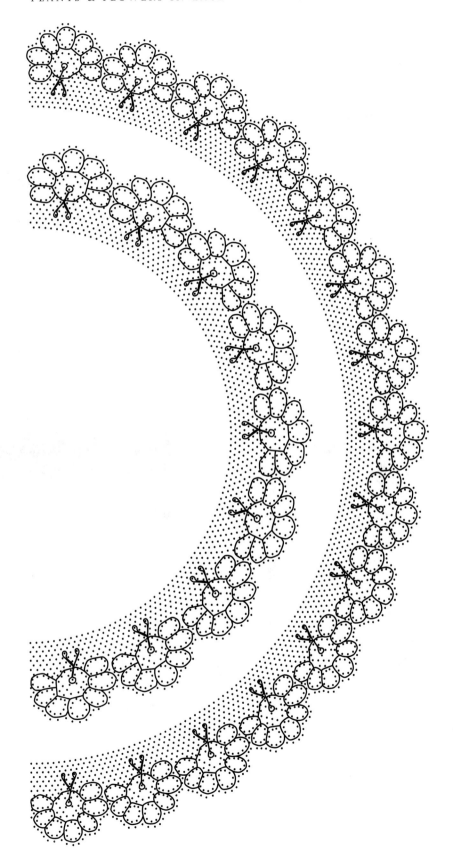

Wild Rose Motif

Bridget M. Cook UK

Bobbins: 74 pairs
6 pairs of gimps
Thread: 120/2 cotton
DMC 16 for the gimps

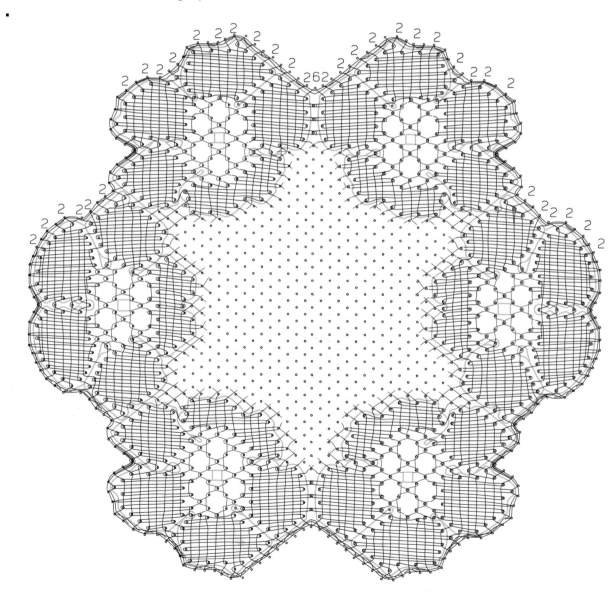

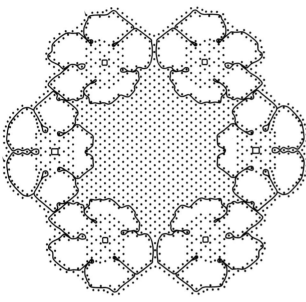

Flowered Handkerchief

Pat Milne Australia

Bobbins: 19 pairs
            1 pair of gimps
Thread: Retors d'Alsace 50 (Broder Machine 50)
            DMC Cotton Perlé 8 for the gimp

Dieppe ground: halfstitch, pin, halfstitch and twist
Headside: use extra twists to ensure a firm headside

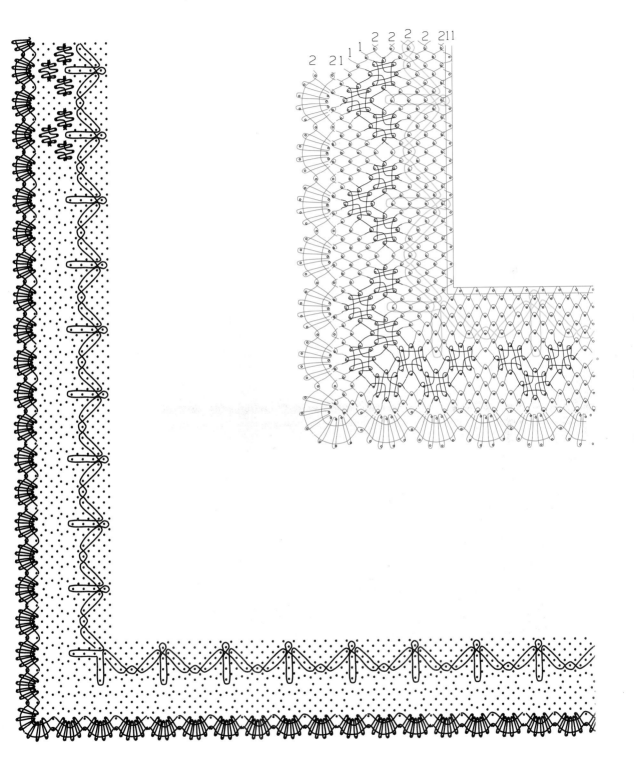

Wheat Ear Earrings

Glenda Howell New Zealand

Bobbins: 12 pairs

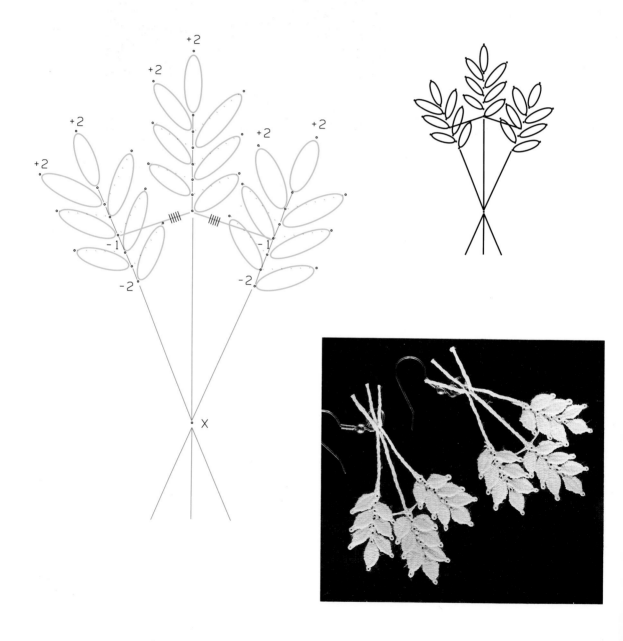

Small White Rose Flower Motif

Thread: 40/2 linen

Glenda Howell New Zealand

Bobbins: 9 pairs
Thread: 50/2 linen

Suitable for large paperweights

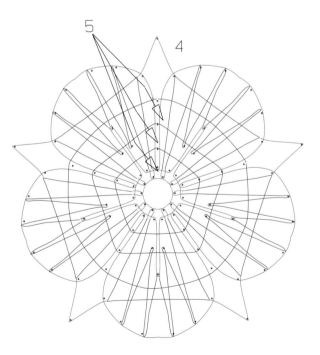

Flower Miniatures

Liz Tibbetts UK

Thread: Brok Cotton 100/2
Coarse thread: Coats Traditional soft cotton

*All these motifs are suitable for jewellery
or small frames
1. Snowdrop
2. Toadstool
Pin and stitch filling with random leadworks
used to imitate the spots on the red-and-white Fly
Agaric toadstool
3. Daffodil*

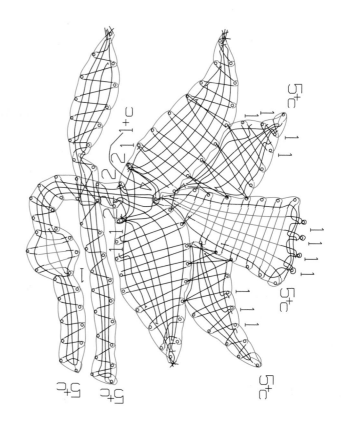

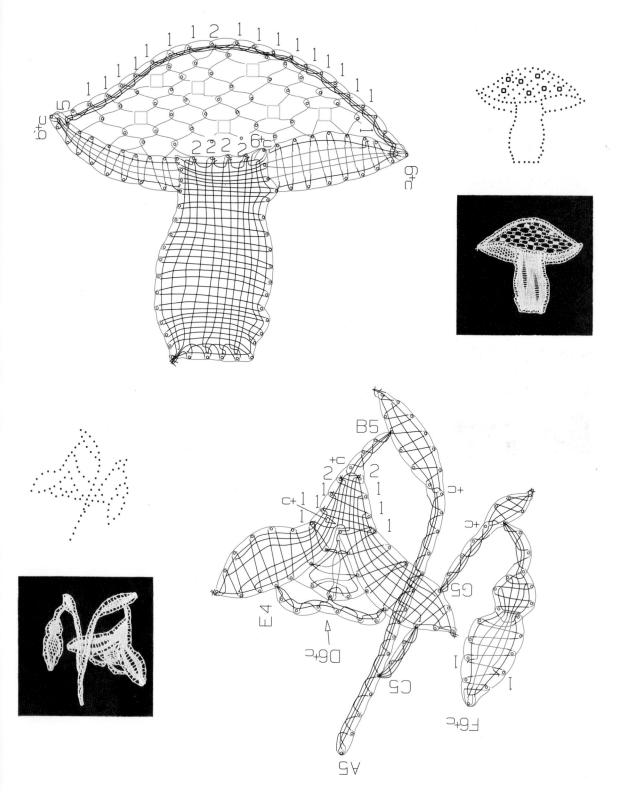

Harebells

Liz Tibbetts UK

Thread: Brok Cotton 120/2
Coarse thread: Coats Traditional soft cotton

The larger motif is suitable for a paperweight;
the smaller is suitable for jewellery.

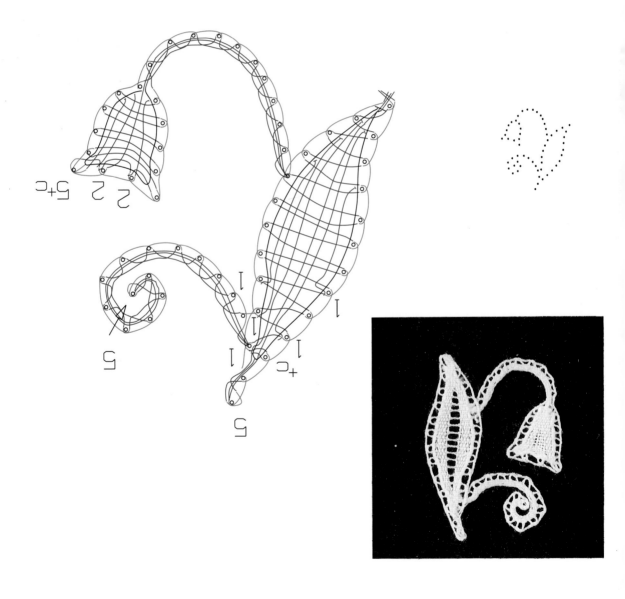

5+c 2 2 2

5

5

6+c

Daisy Chains

Liz Tibbetts UK

Thread: Brok Cotton 100/2
Coarse thread: Coats traditional soft cotton

*Singly suitable for jewellery or in chains as a
frame or bookmark: for clarity the diagram on
the opposite page is in two halves.*

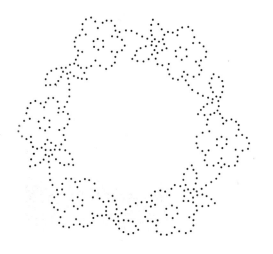

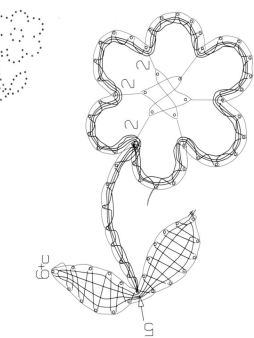

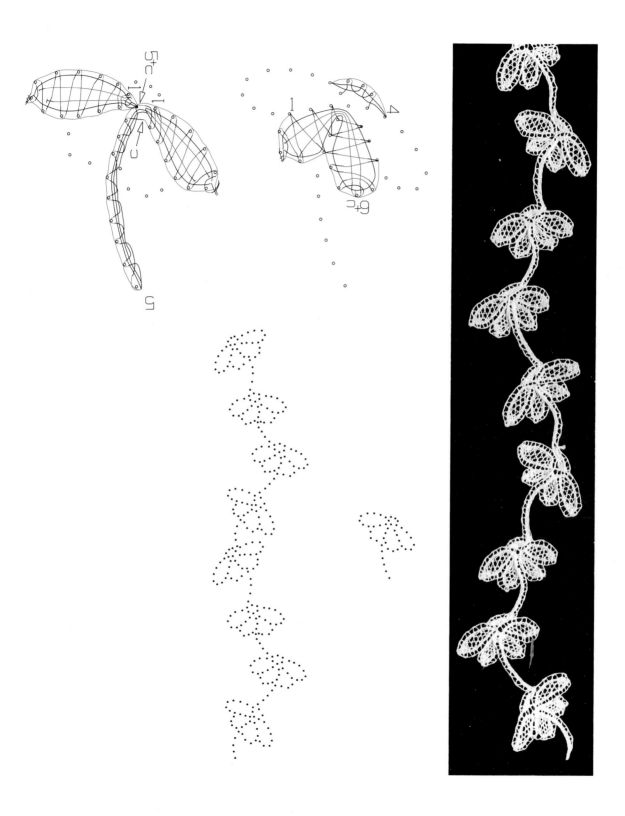

Tiny Fruits and Flowers

Liz Tibbetts UK

Thread: Brok Cotton 120/2
Coarse thread: Coats Traditional soft cotton

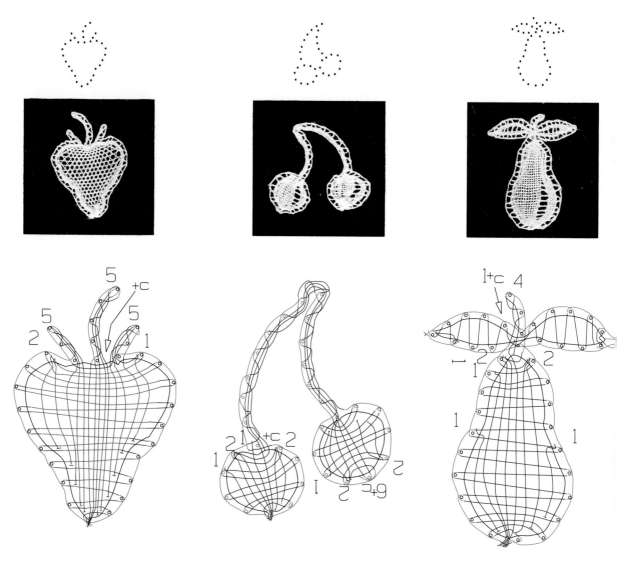

All these motifs are suitable for pendants and brooches
1. Strawberry 2. Cherries 3. Pear 4. Snowdrop 5. Mushroom 6. Leaf and tendril

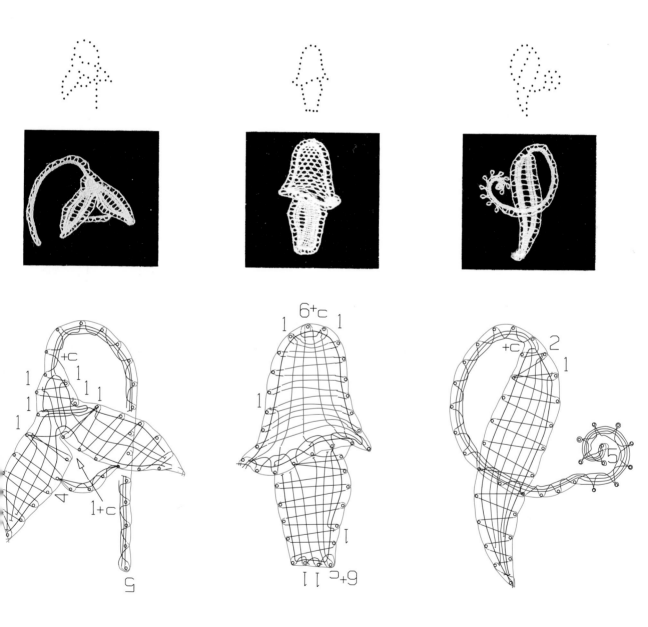

Tulips

Liz Tibbetts UK

Thread: Brok Cotton 120/2
Coarse thread: Coats Traditional soft cotton

*The larger tulip is designed as a bookmark,
but the flower head can be used on its own
for jewellery.*

Start the stem at A and B.

*After the divisions, work up to C and D,
and then temporarily leave the pairs.
Work leaf E and sew out.
Return to C and finish leaf, then return to D
and finish leaf.*

*At the two points marked "X", all the pairs
are bunched together and the whole is twisted
once.*

*For clarity the two halfstitch sections of the
tulip F and G are joined and then continued
down the stem.*

Lastly work H, I, J, and K.

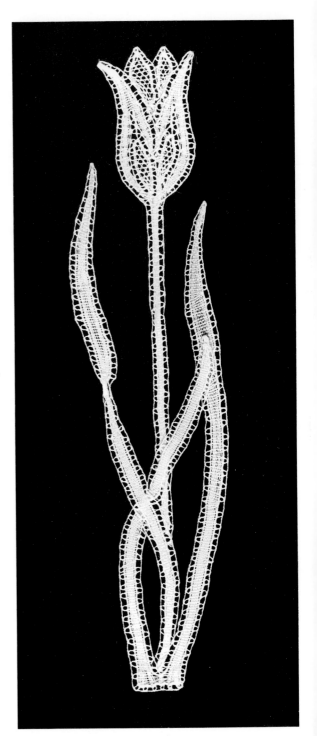

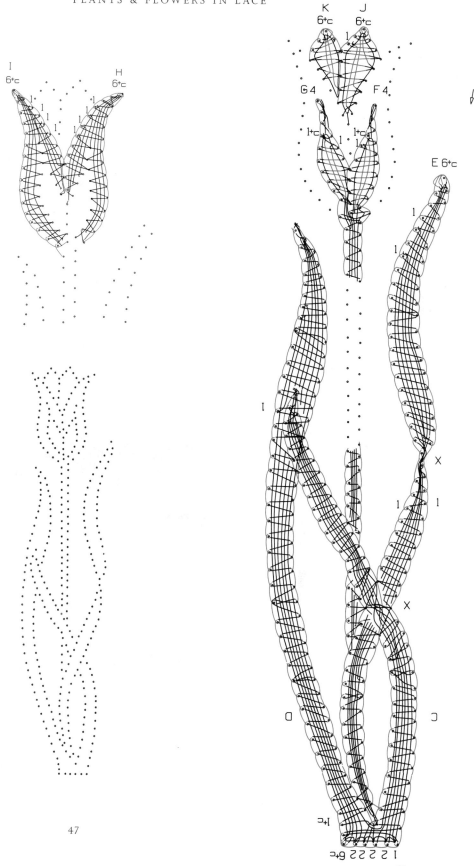

Sources of information

UNITED KINGDOM

The Lace Guild
The Hollies
53 Audnam
Stourbridge
West Midlands DY8 4AE

OIDFA
Tamara Golding
'Nonsuch Too'
27 Ollands Road
Reepham
Norfolk
NR10 4EL

**The British College
of Lace**
21 Hillmorton Road
Rugby
Warwickshire CV22 5DF

International Old Lacers
Ann Keller
Cool Valley
Abingdon Park
Shankill
Dublin

The Lacemakers' Circle
20 Ulverscroft Road
Loughborough
Leicester
LE11 3PU

The Lace Society
Lynwood
Stratford Road
Oversley, Alcester
Warwickshire B49 6PG

Ring of Tatters
Miss B. Netherwood
269 Oregon Way
Chaddesden
Derby DE21 6UR

AUSTRALIA

Australian Lace Guild
National Committee
Box Hill
Victoria 3128

Australian Lace
Magazine
P.O. Box 609
Manly
NSW 2095

BELGIUM

OIDFA
Alice de Smedt
Welvaartstraat 149
B 9300 Aalst
Alg. Spaar-en-Lijfentekas

**Belgische
Kantorganisatie**
Irma Boone
Gentse Steenweg 296
B-9240 Zele

FRANCE

OIDFA
Suzanne Puech
3 Chemin de Parenty
F-69250 Neuville sur
Saône

GERMANY

OIDFA
Uta Ulrich
Papenbergweg 33
D-32756 Detmold

**Deutscher
Klöppelverband
e.V**
Schulstr. 38
D-52531
Übach Palenberg

**Klöppelschule
Nordhalben**
Klöppelschule 4
D-96365 Nordhalben

THE NETHERLANDS

OIDFA
Elly De Vries
Couwenhoven 52-07
NL-3703 ER Zeist

LOKK
Boterbloem 56
NL-7322 GX Apeldoorn

SWITZERLAND

**Fédération de
Dentellières**
Suisses
Evelyne Lütolf
Buhnstrasse 12
CH-8052 Zürich

USA

OIDFA
Elaine Merritt
5915 Kyburz Place
San José CA 95120

International Old Lacers
Editor
Julie Hendrick
2737 NE 98th
Seattle WA 98115

**Point Ground Tours &
Publications**
124 W. Irvington Place
Denver
Co 80223-1539

OIDFA
(International Bobbin
and Needle
Lace Organization)

President
Lydia Thiels-Mertens
Jagersberg 1
B-3294 Molenstede-
Diest
Belgium

Vice President
Alice De Smedt
Welvaartstraat 149
B 9300 Aalst
Belgium